An African tale

Rain

the
BIG
PICTURE

D1080694

Catherine Chambers

Published 2010 by
A&C Black Publishers Ltd.
36 Soho Square, London, W1D 3QY

www.acblack.com

ISBN HB 978-1-4081-2795-7
     PB 978-1-4081-3154-1

Produced for A&C Black by Calcium. www.calciumcreative.co.uk

Printed and bound in China by C&C Offset Printing Co.

Acknowledgements

The publishers would like to thank the following for their kind permission to reproduce their photographs:

Cover: Corbis: Gianni Giansanti (front); Fotolia: Maria Adelaide Silva (back). **Pages:** Alamy Images: Wayne Hutchinson 16, Giles Moberly 18-19; Corbis: Ed Kashi 11, 14-15; Fotolia: Aureleiii 2-3, Denis Cordier 6, Maria Adelaide Silva 6-7; Shutterstock: Anton Albert 4, Andrew Chin 14-15, Lucian Coman 20-21, Dainis Derics 4-5, 20-21, Fonats 8-9, Gkuna 16-17, JCPJR 10-11, Gregor Kervina 1, Muriel Lasure 3, 12, 12-13, Chris Leachman 17, Frances A. Miller 22-23, Louie Schoeman 24, Konstantin Sutyagin 9, Tish1 18-19, Yaro 7.

Contents

Rain 4

Dusty Days 6

Will it Rain? 8

Rain at Last! 10

Time to Farm 12

Danger! 14

Drying Out 16

No More Rain 18

Dry Again 20

Glossary 22

Further Reading 23

Index 24

Rain

We cannot live without rain. It helps our crops to grow and gives us water to drink.

Meet Adamu

*"I live in a country called Nigeria, in **Africa**. It is often dry where I live."*

How much?

Some parts of Africa have too much rain. Other parts do not have enough. Very little rain falls in the part of Nigeria where Adamu lives.

Hi!

Find out about rain where I live.

Dusty Days

It doesn't rain in winter where Adamu lives. Instead, the weather stays dry.

Adamu says

*"It is January and very dry. A cold wind blows from the sandy, red Sahara **desert**. It carries a lot of red dust."*

The wind covers Adamu's village in red dust.

Dry rivers

By March, the dusty ground is cracking. Rivers are dry. It is hard for Adamu's family to water their tomato and pepper crops.

Dry, dry, dry

Will it Rain?

In April, the people in Adamu's village wait for it to rain.

Adamu says

"Now a different wind is blowing dark storm clouds from the ocean to my village. When they get here, it will rain."

A storm is coming

Rain clouds

Rain falls gently from pale grey clouds. When there is a storm, rain pours from dark clouds.

Everyone is waiting for the rain.

Rain at Last!

Dark rain clouds race towards Adamu's village. The clouds are heavy and wet. It starts to rain.

Adamu says

"My family loves the rain. The rain will water the dry ground. I think the thunder and lightning are scary! I run inside to hide."

Flash! Bang!

Food to eat

The rain means that Adamu's family can start to grow crops, so they will have food to eat.

Adamu's mother is happy now the rain is here.

11

Time to Farm

It is May. Because of the rain, the earth is red and damp. It is time to start farming!

Adamu says

*"My family sows crop **seeds** in long piles of soil. Deep dips between the piles hold the rainwater."*

*Cattle **plough** the soil so it is ready for the seeds.*

We grow...

Adamu's family sows **maize** and **millet** seeds and groundnuts. Groundnuts are tasty peanuts. They grow under the ground.

Wet, wet, wet

Danger!

It is June, and the rain still falls. It fills the rivers. If too much rain falls, the rivers may flood.

Adamu says

"My father and I travel to the city to buy more seeds. The rain has fallen so heavily that the roads are flooded."

Heavy rain makes the dirt roads muddy.

Too much rain

Lights out

Lightning can hit **power stations** during rainstorms. With no **electricity**, people can have no light and power for days.

Drying Out

In September, the rain is light. The land slowly dries out. It is time to sow vegetable seeds.

Adamu says

"My family grows vegetables in a small, wet field near the river. It is called a fadama."

Hoe, hoe, hoe

The soil is dug with a **hoe** before the seeds are planted.

We plant...

Adamu's family plants tomatoes, spinach, **okra**, sweet peppers, and onions in the field. Bananas are sometimes planted too.

No More Rain

It is October. There will be no more rain now until next year. The crops have dried in the sun.

Adamu says

"It is time to **harvest** the crops. Drummers play music to help everyone work. Harvest time is fun!"

Drummers play to celebrate the harvest.

Harvest time

People in Adamu's village harvest millet and maize crops. The **grain** from the crops can be made into flour for food such as bread and cereal.

Work to the beat!

Dry Again

It is December. A dry wind blows from the Sahara again. Everything is covered in red dust once more.

Adamu says

"We do not farm during the winter when there is no rain. This means I can go to school."

Whoosh!

Water to last

Adamu's village has a **well**. The villagers use water from the well during the dry season when there is no rain.

Now Adamu has time for schoolwork – and play!

21

Glossary

Africa large area of land with many countries

crops plants people grow for food

desert hot, dry, dusty or rocky place

electricity power for lights and machines

flood when water breaks out of a river and spreads onto land around the river

grain small seed of a plant

harvest to cut down or pick crops

hoe tool used to dig up soil

maize crop that is made into flour

millet crop that is made into flour

okra long, thin, green vegetable

plough to dig up and turn over soil

power station place where power such as electricity is made

seeds parts of a plant from which new plants grow

well hole in the ground where water is stored

Further Reading

Websites

Find out how rain is made at:
www.kidzone.ws/water

Play the rain games at:
www.metoffice.gov.uk/education/kids

Books

A is for Africa by Ifeoma Onyefulu,
World Alphabet Publications (1996).

Drought (Wild Weather) by Catherine Chambers,
Heinemann Library (2008).

Nigeria (Looking at Countries) by Jillian Powell,
Franklin Watts (2007).

Index

clouds 9, 10
crops 4, 7, 11, 12–13, 17,
    18–19

desert 6
drummers 18
dust 6–7, 20

fadama 16
farm 12–13, 16–17, 18–19,
    20
floods 14
food 11, 13, 17, 19

grain 19
groundnuts 13

harvest 18–19
hoe 16

lightning 10, 15

maize 13, 19
millet 13, 19

Nigeria 4–5

okra 17

plough 12

rivers 7
roads 14

Sahara 6, 20
seeds 12, 14, 16
storm 8–9, 10

water 4, 21
well 21
wind 6, 8, 20